Kwanzaa

by Sheila Anderson
illustrated by Holli Conger

Content Consultant: Dr. Pamela R. Frese
Professor of Anthropology, College of Wooster

magic Wagon

visit us at www.abdopublishing.com

Published by Magic Wagon, a division of the ABDO Group, 8000 West 78th Street, Edina, Minnesota 55439. Copyright © 2010 by Abdo Consulting Group, Inc. International copyrights reserved in all countries. All rights reserved. No part of this book may be reproduced in any form without written permission from the publisher.

Looking Glass Library™ is a trademark and logo of Magic Wagon.

Printed in the United States.

Text by Sheila Anderson
Illustrations by Holli Conger
Edited by Mari Kesselring
Interior layout and design by Becky Daum
Cover design by Becky Daum

Library of Congress Cataloging-in-Publication Data
Anderson, Sheila.
  Kwanzaa / by Sheila Anderson ; illustrated by Holli Conger ; content consultant, Pamela R. Frese.
     p. cm. — (Cultural holidays)
  Includes index.
  ISBN 978-1-60270-604-0
  1. Kwanzaa. 2. African Americans—Social life and customs. I. Frese, Pamela R. II. Conger, Holli, ill. III. Title.
  GT4403.A52 2010
  394.2612—dc22
                                    2008050548

Table of Contents

What Is Kwanzaa?

On December 26, many families begin a celebration of African heritage. It is called Kwanzaa. Kwanzaa lasts seven days.

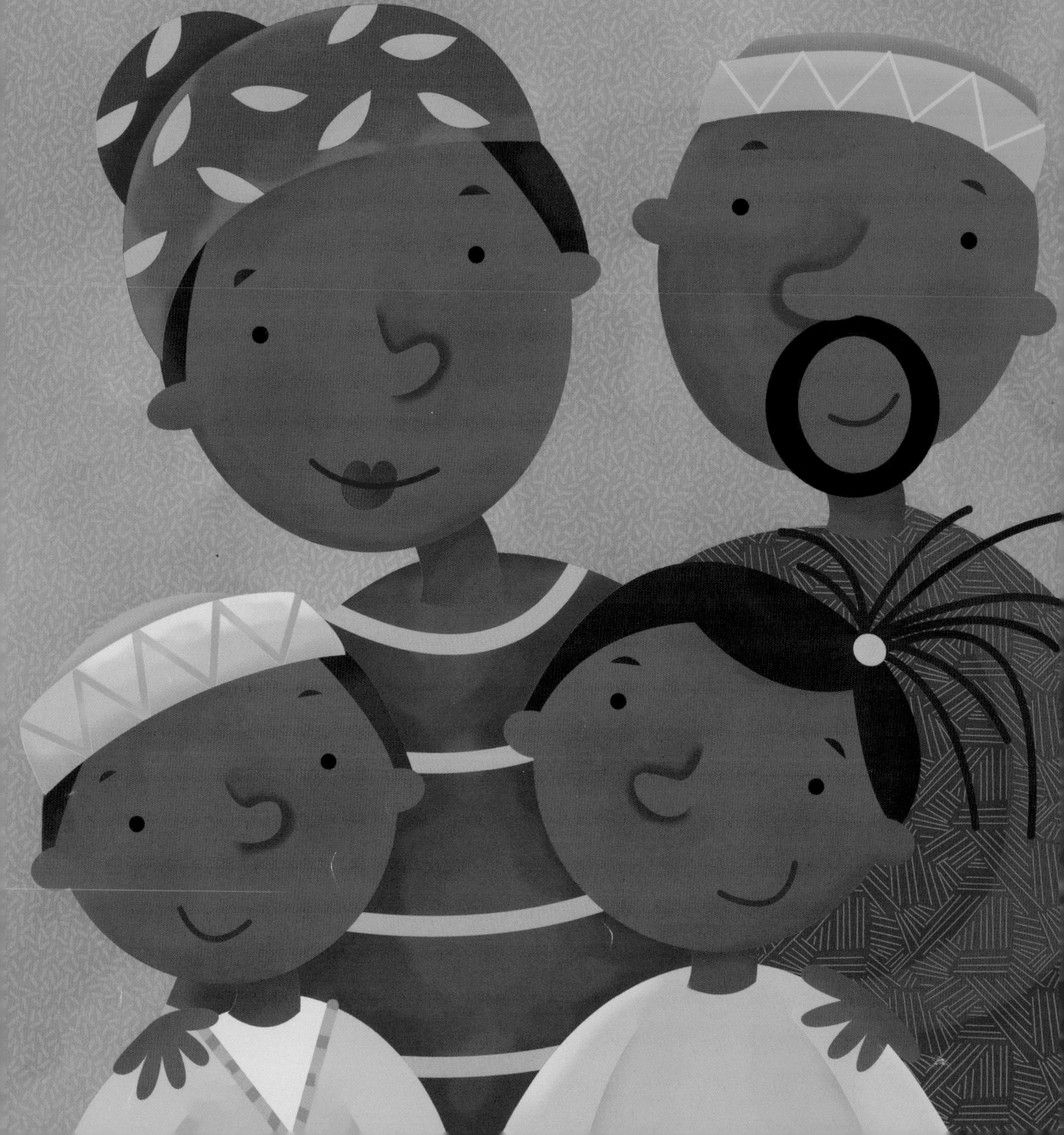

The word *Kwanzaa* comes from the Swahili saying *matunda ya kwanza*. It means "first fruits." Swahili is a language. It is spoken in many areas of Africa.

During Kwanzaa, people are encouraged to wear African clothing, jewelry, and hairstyles. Women might wear clothes made from colorful African cloth. Men often dress in black, red, and green.

Joyous Kwanzaa!

In Africa, people gather to celebrate the harvest of crops. This is when the food that people have grown is ready to be picked. These are called the "first fruits." It is a time to celebrate. Everyone is thankful for the food.

Kwanzaa is similar to harvest celebrations. It is a time to be thankful. People give thanks for their family, community, and African heritage.

Although Kwanzaa is a celebration of African heritage, anyone can celebrate Kwanzaa. People who celebrate Kwanzaa may also celebrate Christmas.

Principles of Kwanzaa

During Kwanzaa, people remember seven African principles. Each day of Kwanzaa, people focus on one principle.

During Kwanzaa, people greet each other using the Swahili language. Someone will ask, "What's the news?" in Swahili. The answer will be the Swahili word for the principle of the day. For example, they might say *umoja*. This is the Swahili word for "unity."

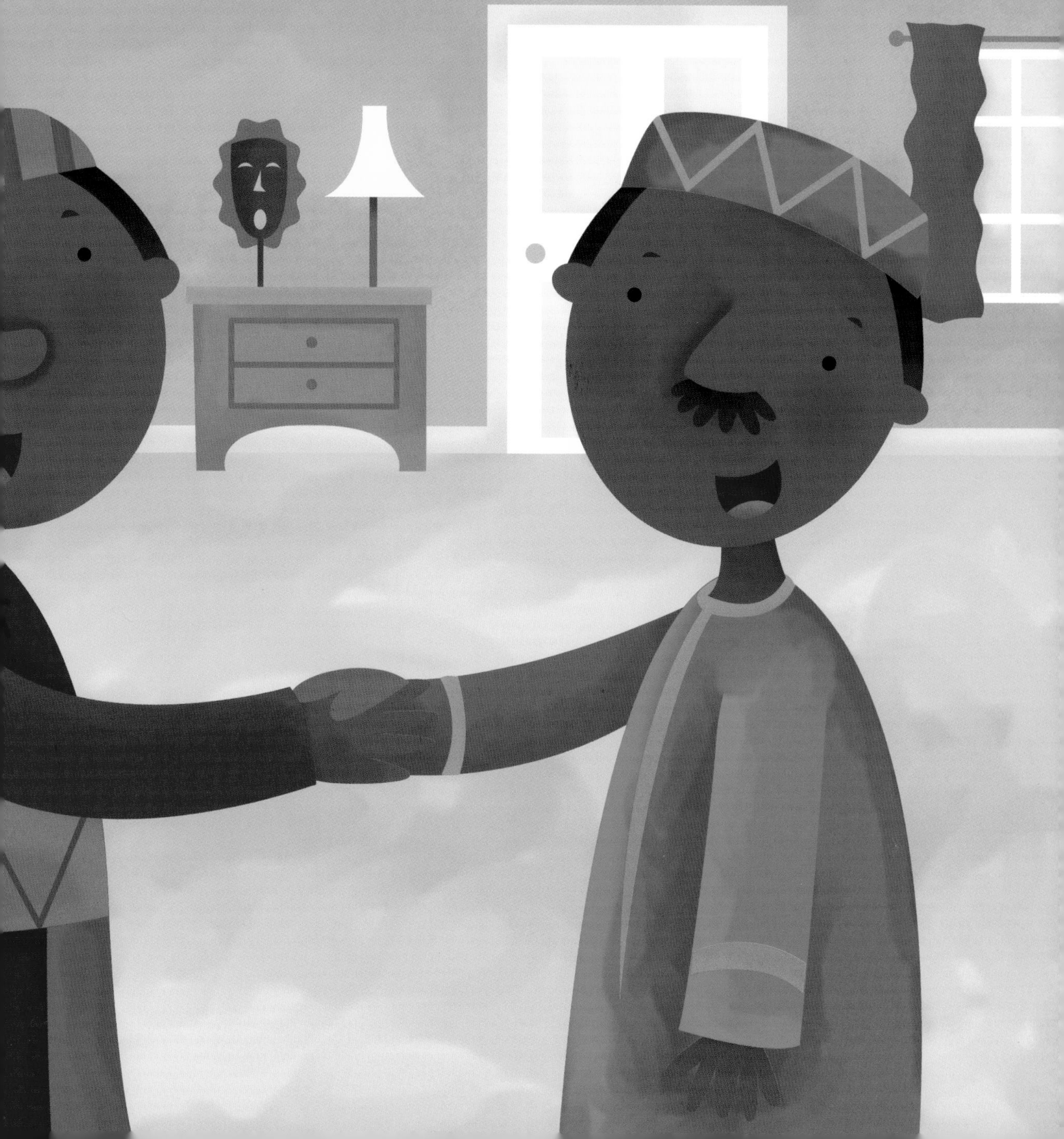

Kwanzaa begins on December 26. On this day people focus on umoja or "unity." They try to work together. In the United States, they celebrate the oneness of the African-American community.

On December 27, people focus on *kujichagulia*. This word means "self-determination." It is about showing who you are through your words and actions. For example, caring for your siblings shows that you are responsible.

On December 28, the focus is on *ujima*. This means "collective work and responsibility." People think of ways they can work together and help their community.

December 29 is the day to focus on *ujamaa*.
Ujamaa means "cooperative economics."
People shop at stores owned by people in their
community. This helps strengthen the community.

On December 30, people focus on *nia*. This means "purpose." People are reminded to develop strong African-American communities. This means being proud of African history and culture.

December 31 is the day to celebrate *kuumba*. This means "creativity." This day teaches people to make their communities beautiful. One way people do this is by cleaning their homes.

The last day of Kwanzaa is January 1. This day's focus is on *imani*. Imani means "faith." It teaches people to trust, honor, and believe in their parents, teachers, leaders, and culture.

Decorations

Each night of Kwanzaa, the family gathers around a special place setting. The place setting contains seven items.

The first object on the Kwanzaa table is a place mat. It stands for African history and tradition. On top of the mat are ears of corn, a candleholder, candles, crops (fruits and vegetables), a cup, and gifts.

Many families include a flag in their Kwanzaa decorations. The flag has three horizontal stripes: one black, one red, and one green. It is also common to hang a poster of the seven principles.

Each item on the Kwanzaa place setting stands for something. Ears of corn stand for children in the family. If a family does not have children, it still displays an ear of corn. Corn is a symbol of community upbringing. This means that everyone in the community helps raise the children.

The candleholder stands for the original plant from which all people come. It holds seven candles. The candles are black, red, and green. Black represents the people. Red stands for the people's struggles. Green represents the future and the hope that comes from people's struggles.

The candles are always put in the candleholder in a special order. The black candle is in the middle. The three red candles are to the left of the black candle. The three green candles are to the right of the black candle.

The crops stand for the work people do and the results of that work. Next to these is a cup. It is a symbol of unity.

Lastly, a family may display gifts. Usually the gifts are from parents to their children. These gifts reward children for their accomplishments. They also encourage children to be successful in the coming year. Common gifts are African art and books about African Americans.

Celebrations Today

Each night of Kwanzaa, the family has a special dinner. Before dinner, the Kwanzaa candles are lit. On the first day of Kwanzaa, someone lights the black candle. On the second day, the black candle is lit again. And then, the first red candle is lit. On the third day, the first green candle is also lit. One more candle is lit each night.

Each candle stands for the principle of the day. The person lighting the candle names that day's principle and gives an example of it.

On December 31, families have a big feast. Everyone brings food to share. Traditional foods include shrimp gumbo or sweet potato pie. The party might include drumming or storytelling. These activities can be part of any day's Kwanzaa celebration. They are especially included on December 31.

The last day of Kwanzaa is a day of rest. People make goals for the future. What goals would you make during Kwanzaa?

Glossary

culture—a group's common language, customs, dress, art, religion, and way of living.

goals—things someone wants to accomplish or complete.

heritage—the culture of our ancestors.

symbol—something that stands for something else.

tradition—customs, ideas, and beliefs handed down from one generation to the next.

On the Web

To learn more about Kwanzaa, visit ABDO Group online at **www.abdopublishing.com**. Web sites about Kwanzaa are featured on our Book Links page. These links are routinely monitored and updated to provide the most current information available.

Index

3/11